St. Thérèse of Lisieux

NIETZSCHE IS MY BROTHER

A Play

by

Bridget Edman, OCD

ICS Publications
Institute of Carmelite Studies
Washington, DC

2010

ICS Publications
2131 Lincoln Road. NE
Washington, D.C. 20002-1199
(800) 832-8489
www. icspublications.org

Cover Design by Rosemary Moak, OCDS

Typeset and Produced in the United States of America

Library of Congress Cataloging-in-Publication Data
    Edman, Bridget
    [Roses have thorns]
    Nietzche is my brother: a play by Bridget Edman
       p. cm.
    Originally published under title: Roses have thorns: Washington,
    D.C.: ICS Publications, 2002
    ISBN 978-0-935216-79-0
    1. Title
    PR9369.4E46R67 2010
    822'92 —dc22
        2010002217

Table of Contents

Introduction to Bridget Edman's
Nietzsche Is My Brother

Adapted from Joan FitzGerald

The Church has always paid attention to those "afar," to those who do not go to church, who perhaps know very little or nothing at all about it. The mission of evangelization which has been going on in these past years is full of initiatives taken in the attempts to reach those who are usually outside the reach of the Church, with a spirit that is anything but proselytizing, ready to listen, to understand, rather than to "preach" in the conventional sense. This openness characterizes the play by Sister Bridget Edman, which has won the first prize in the International Competition for Religious Drama, a play thought out and written in Cape Town, far from the center of the Church but imbued with the same spirit which the Catholic Church as a whole embraces.

The author of this play "Nietzsche Is My Brother" is an enclosed Carmelite nun, who joined the Carmelites in South Africa after a personal religious quest which took her from her native Sweden, and the Lutheran Church in which she grew up and for which she worked – first at home, then in Holland and England, and finally in South Africa – where, in 1977, she left the Protestant faith to join the Catholic Church, and the year after, the Order of the Discalced Carmelites. Since then she has always lived in the Carmelite convent, first in Johannesburg, and then, when that convent closed, in Cape Town.

What interests Sister Edman, both in her articles[1] (which not by chance deal with Thérèse's "dark night of the soul") and in this play, is

---

[1]   "Thérèse and the Dark Night", *Spiritual Life*, vol. 43, no. 3 (Fall 1997), 170-179 and "St Thérèse of Lisieux, Saint of the Twenty-first Century?", *Mount Carmel,* vol. 46, no. 1 (April-June 1998), 31-40.

the problem of faith which is characteristic of modern man. That she has written an article on St John of the Cross and the Existentialists and another comparing the same saint to Kierkegaard, seems logical enough to one who has compared St Thérèse of the Child Jesus and Friedrich Nietzsche as she has done in *Nietzsche Is My Brother.* Up to now Sister Edman has written a couple of plays for private circulation only, that is, among her sisters in Christ, of which one seems to develop along lines fairly similar to the text we have before us, having put together Confucius, Plato and St John of the Cross: unfortunately for us, we cannot read it, for the sisters did not keep a copy. At this very moment, she is undertaking a new play which is only apparently on a different topic, the student uprisings at the end of the Sixties. As she writes, "it too deals with the great questions of life ... but this time in a modern setting, being anchored in the student revolt and idealism of the sixties and then what happened to the 'idealists' twenty-five years later."

This information, though scanty, allows us to put into focus the themes which interest this playwright: the search for truth in which modern man is engaged: his incessant quest for meaning in life, and the comparison with those who have received an answer to their questions "in the infinite mystery of God, stretching out His hand to us in Jesus Christ."[2] Comparison, not contrast: essential to Edman's thinking and effectively dramatized in *Nietzsche Is My Brother,* is her rejection of any kind of condescension on the part of the believer towards the unbeliever. What we find instead is a humble and profound recognition of the existential search which they share: the precariousness of faith from which no-one is exempt, neither the atheist who finds no answer to his questions, nor the Christian when he encounters the silence of God, and, crossing the desert of total uncertainty, can only trust Him, without any guarantee that He is there or that He is listening.

It is this shared experience, of silence and darkness, of pre-

---

[2]   The quotations are from personal letters from the author to me.

cariousness, which Sister Edman dramatises in her text, putting into *action*, and not merely into words, that spirit of openness towards those "afar" that, as I said earlier, is one of the characteristics of the Church's evangelization..

The structure of *Nietzsche Is My Brother* deliberately calls to mind a musical score rather than a play: we note that the division is not into acts and scenes but into "movements," five of them, to be precise (thus recalling, however, canonical Renaissance drama), each of which is accompanied by part of the corresponding movement in Mahler's tenth symphony. Each "movement" enacts parallel episodes freely taken from the lives of Saint Thérèse of Lisieux and Friedreich Nietzsche, in which they express their developing characteristic thought. There is obviously nothing "realistic" in all this, since, though the two were practically contemporaries (Thérèse lived from 1873 to 1897, Nietzsche from 1844 to 1900, but by 1888 he had already gone mad), neither of them knew anything about the other, nor does the play have biographical pretensions. Instead it takes its cue from events in the lives of both which are likely, rather than historically "correct". This Thérèse and this Nietzsche are dramatic creations – highly dramatic, at that, in which the essence of the historical Thérèse and the historical Nietzsche is distilled. The method by which they are presented, is, to be true, realistic enough, but within well-defined limits. And at the end of the third and fifth movements realism gives way to lyricism, in two scenes in which Thérèse and Nietzsche meet on an ideal plane, a plane where communication takes place both in and despite of the short, almost choral phrases of dialogue that remind one of certain moments in Beckett's plays.

I said that the play is structured according to parallel scenes in the lives of the two main characters, but not in a strict sense, in that if in the first two movements of scenes centered on Thérèse alternate with others centered on Nietzsche, the scheme is anything but rigid. The third movement begins with Thérèse alone, on a totally dark stage, knocking, calling out, and receiving no answer, thus putting on stage in physical and visual terms that "trial" which was (and would be to the end of her life) the real "dark night" of her soul. And it is not by chance that the scenes with Thérèse are more crowded, more full of other people, than those of Nietzsche, as if to underline his loneliness, his lack of human contacts, especially as we come close to his final madness.

But parallelism is not merely a theatrical technique to make the spectator compare the two characters: it reflects parallel realities in their spiritual lives, in the search for truth which marks these two figures. Against Nietzsche's "will to power", which he emphasises on stage in a scene with his secretary Peter Gast (alluding, as he does a great deal of the time, to *Thus Spoke Zarathustra*) the playwright contraposes Thérèse's "will to believe," which we intuit in her ordeal and in her dialogue with the atheist doctor who comes to examine her and who is the only one who can understand her, that will which she expresses in *The Story of a Soul* when she writes "I sing only that which I WANT TO BELIEVE"[3] Nietzsche reiterates his theory of the Superman and his scorn for the weak (especially women, whom he calls "animals" – we are clearly in the period of his life after his failed love-affair with Lou Salomé); Thérèse instead extols "littleness" and makes of it her "little way." And Nietzsche's final madness, which is dramatised in the final movement, can be contrasted with that which Thérèse calls *her* madness: "ma folie à moi, c'est ésperer"[4]

But even these are only parallels to a certain point: Nietszche's life, as we know, follows a very different path to Thérèse's, and the play makes no attempt to force a likeness where there is none nor to try and make the two roads forcibly meet. Thérèse hears voices mocking her, telling her that her longed-for death will bring her an even darker night, "la nuit du néant"[5] - and the same night in which

---

[3]   Thérèse of Lisieux, *Story of a Soul* Ms. C translated by John Clarke ocd

Nietzsche is groping – but she not only accepts her "épreuve" *(trial)* but embraces this opportunity to "eat at the same table" with atheists, for the salvation of their souls.[6] What the playwright does is to render this "opening" towards unbelievers theatrically dramatic, inventing the free-thinking doctor who comes to visit the sick, then dying, Thérèse, and talks to her on subjects which would cause scandal to her sisters, if they but knew of these conversations; but it is precisely these conversations which create an opportunity for Thérèse to open herself up towards the great proportion of humankind that she knew nothing of till then, and, at the same time, forges a relationship of mutual esteem between her and the doctor.

These dialogues between people so different from each other – between Thérèse and the doctor in realistic terms, between Thérèse and Nietzsche in more symbolic ones, are the key to the play. Dialogue means opening oneself up to the other, not only talking, but *listening*, and we understand why Sister Edman felt the need to write not another article, but a play on these two figures. This also sheds light on the importance of the two scenes where Thérèse and Nietzsche ideally meet, through a bare, simple dialogue, focusing on just a few things: the invitation to be together, not to take refuge, defensively, in solitude, to go somewhere together – where, she doesn't know, it doesn't matter, even to fall into the abyss, as long as they do it together. When, as promised, Thérèse returns, immediately after her death, to encounter a Nietzsche who is by now mad, her invitation is more explicit: the places to go to are beautiful (mountains), the things to do (play the violin) also. Nietzsche seems to awaken not so much to a religious conversion but to the possibility that solidarity, company, love itself, exists, and that they may find, even pick, roses – roses without thorns,

---

4   ibid. "My madness, is to hope"
5   ibid. "The night of nothingness"
6   ibid.

for roses have thorns only inside us, and where Thérèse and Nietzsche are going there is no longer any suffering. But even here, nothing is forced: we leave Nietzsche fascinated, but still undecided, with Thérèse inviting him to go with her, and he begging her to stay, and the dialogue continues with a dying fall, until in the silence of human voices we hear the Resurrection motif in Mahler's symphony.

The play does not point to a resolution, and ending. Sister Edman deliberately leaves suspended in mid-air the "answer" to modern man's drama, which may or may not be found in Christian faith. The reader and the spectator leave this fictional world, but with a strong sense of involvement – in one way or another, their own faith, their own thoughts and their own feelings have been called into question. The questions which the two characters ask themselves are not relevant only to their own times, their own world, but involved all humanity today. And as Sister Edman notes, the question "where do we come from, where are we going?" is one we all ask ourselves. The importance of this play is that it asks this question in dramatic, theatrical, terms, not just of the main characters, but of the audience who has seen --- who has taken part in --- *Nietzsche Is My Brother.*

Nietzsche Is My Brother

"To every man his death."
(Martin Heidegger)

Drama in five movements.
Music: Gustav Mahler's 10th Symphony

Bridget Edman OCD

The music, Mahler's 10th symphony, can be used as indicated or it may be used ad lib, according to the judgement of the producer. However, some part of the respective movement should be played at the corresponding movement in the play. It could, though, be much reduced and only played as soft background music.

CHARACTERS

St Thérèse

Mother Agnès }

Sr Geneviève (Céline)   } Thérèse's sisters

Mother Marie de Gonzague

An old nun

A doctor

Nietzsche

Peter Gast

A maid

Franziska Nietzsche

MOVEMENT ONE

(Music begins before curtain opens, then gradually fades.)

*(The scene is a library, typical Jugend furnishing, semi-lit.
On a small side-table is a rose in a vase.
Nietzsche sits at his desk, writing.)*

(Church bells are heard in the far distance.)

NIETZSCHE: That noise! Every night the same! Let them pray if that makes them happy, but do not disturb everybody else. *(The bells are ringing in the back-ground.)*

I too was a pious boy once. The pastor's son. But he died – then I went to boarding school – and then – I was always alone. I could not fit in. I never can. It was like an ice castle. I tried to smash, to burn – We must smash, smash – smash everything to pieces, until nothing remains.
Only the fighter will win. – I shall fight. I will show them. – I will show him that I can win.
I need nobody. Neither man, nor woman, least of all woman, nor God. When I needed them they left me, one by one. My father died, woman betrayed me. God hid himself, and then He died too. So I will go it alone. Alone. I will fight alone to the top. Too bad for them if they do not understand my genius. –

But it is fearsome. It is cold and lonely. Nothing remains. Nothing, not even suicide. *(Gets up.)*

I will away – and henceforth I trust in myself and in my own hands. Open lies the sea, my Genoese ship surges onward into the blue. – Everything glitters new and newer, noontide sleeps on space and time: your eye alone – dreadfully it gazes upon me, infinity! –
My infinity is not my father's infinity. It was once but not anymore. My infinity is strong, but I am afraid too. I am afraid, but I must not show it, must not show it. O dreadful infinity. But rather that than hypocrisy, Christian hypocrisy. I have seen enough of that sort. There has been one real Christian, one who was not a hypocrite, and he died on a cross. He had to die on a cross because he was not a hypocrite. He may have been a mad fanatic, but he had the courage of his conviction. He was a noble man, so he had to die, and his teaching died with him. He has followers, alas! who hail him as king and leader, but do they die on a cross? Not they, they make quite sure of that. Slaves, slaves they are and slaves they make. And they are cowards too. When last did you see a courageous Christian? – If I had been a Christian, but I am not!, I would have died on a cross.

The fruit will fall when it is ripe, not before. And fall it must, fall and fall never to return –

(Nietzsche walks around slowly. The light fades almost to darkness.)
Lately I stood at the bridge in the brown night. A song came to me from afar; a golden drop, it welled over the quivering surface. Gondolas, lights, music – drunken it swam out into the twilight *(Music begins in the background)* – My soul, a stringed instrument, invisibly touched sang to itself a gondola song thereto, quivering in many-coloured happiness *(total blackout; music stops)* – Did anyone listen to it?

(Silence, darkness, then music for a short while.)

(Music stops. Full light on a beautiful, romantic monastery garden.)
Sr Thérèse, Mother Agnès are seated on a bench, Sr Geneviève
on a chair. Mother Agnès is making laces, Thérèse and Geneviève
painting. They chat happily as the curtain opens.

THERESE *(giggles)*: This is just like home.

GENEVIEVE: Just miss the chocolate-éclair, hm?

(They all laugh.)

MOTHER AGNES: We were a happy family – so much to be grateful for, when you hear of all the terrible things they do today. All the wicked things Uncle tells us people do, you can hardly believe it. And I am sure he does not tell us the worst. Uncle would not.

(Thérèse and Geneviève look at her.)

THERESE: I wonder if they really are wicked or -?

GENEVIEVE: But surely they must know what is right and what is wrong!

(Thérèse does not look convinced.)

MOTHER AGNES *(looks at Thérèse with a glint in her eyes)*: Perhaps they are just spoilt, as you were.

GENEVIEVE: I presume all sickly children are pampered. But we all loved you to bits.

THERESE: And now?

GENEVIEVE: Ah, you know –

THERESE: But there was not only sunshine. There were clouds too – You remember, when Mama died? It was like a hole in my childhood. Pain or only emptiness? I do not know. Death is strange – She was gone – gone to God, they said. But I wanted God to give her back to me. He did not. *(She smiles.)* Of course in the beauty of heaven – nobody wants to come back, back to the valley of tears – To be with God, to see all, to know all – arrived – destination reached – at home at last – *(looks at the others.)* When I am there, I am going to work, do great work. – I cannot be happy there unless you all come with me, all must come – all sinners too, all pagans – all must come. God loves them and I love them too. *(The others look at her.)* – Unbelievers must come. Everybody must come. Otherwise I will not be happy. – Uncle says there are people – have you heard this? – here in France, today, who say that there is no God or – that you do not know – But, that is impossible! You cannot doubt the existence of God. I do not think they mean it.

GENEVIEVE: Well, they write books about it.

MOTHER AGNES: Have you read any?

GENEVIEVE: No, but I have heard of them.

THERESE: Who told you?

GENEVIEVE: I do not remember, perhaps Uncle or cousin Jacques.

MOTHER AGNES: Thank God you have not read them anyway.

THERESE: But if we do not read these books we do not know what they say.

MOTHER AGNES: We do not need to know that.

THERESE: I think we do.

MOTHER AGNES: You certainly should not worry your little head about these bad things.

THERESE: If I had been a man I would have studied so that I could have known all these things for myself.

MOTHER AGNES: You think too much. It is not good for you. I am afraid you were left too much alone when you were little.

THERESE: And you, who are a Carmelite, say that!

GENEVIEVE: She was not all alone. I was there.

MOTHER AGNES: That is true, of course. – So children, what are we going to do for Mother's feast day?

GENEVIEVE: Nothing.

THERESE: Who writes these books?

MOTHER AGNES: Can you ever forget these books?

THERESE: But if that is what they write today, that is how people think today, and we must know that.

MOTHER AGNES: They are bad people and we do not bother about them.

THERESE: Of course we do! God bothers about them.

MOTHER AGNES: They are wicked.

THERESE: I do not think anybody is wicked.

MOTHER AGNES: But it is wicked to doubt God.

THERESE: I do not think they really doubt. I think they just say so.

GENEVIEVE: Perhaps they cannot help it.

THERESE: Then we must help them. What do they say anyway?

GENEVIEVE: They say that there is no God, everything is just natural.

THERESE: Oh, no! That is terrible. It cannot be true.

MOTHER AGNES: Now we stop this.

(They work in silence for a while.)

THERESE: Do you think, they will let me go to the Missions?

MOTHER AGNES: I do not know. Do you want to?

THERESE: Oh, yes! To travel all around the world to tell all the peoples –

GENEVIEVE: Are you strong enough?

THERESE: I think so – do you not?

GENEVIEVE: I do not know. – *(They look at one another.)*

THERESE *(sings)*:
> Their loss is gain who all forsake
> To find Thy love, O Jesus mine!
> For Thee my ointment jar I break,
> The perfume of my life is Thine!

(They all hum the monotonous tune.)

GENEVIEVE: Well, we travelled to Rome anyway and saw all the famous and holy places: Churches, historical monuments and the beautiful landscape and –

THERESE *(interrupts)*: The people – I learnt a lot. It was like scales falling from my eyes. I remember, I was so young you know, I thought "Is this life?" and I just wanted to run behind Papa, and wished we had been at home again, and that nothing had ever happened. I was so frightened and I never wanted to grow up. I wanted to be little, always to be little. I did not want to know, and yet I knew I had to. I knew I could not go back and be a child again. But it was something I wanted to hold, something I knew must not be lost. What it was, I did not know, but I knew it must not get lost, it was like a treasure. – Do you think one can recapture the innocence of a child?

GENEVIEVE: Of course, in Paradise.

THERESE: Oh, Céline, you are quick with your answers.

MOTHER AGNES: She is right, Thérèse. I do not know why you say such strange things today.

THERESE: Life is strange.

MOTHER AGNES: No, really. I would never have mentioned your pilgrimage if I had known what funny ideas you would come up with.

THERESE: I am glad you spoke of it. – That little group of people on that pilgrimage was like a world in miniature. I saw much, much I would rather not have seen, and yet I am glad I saw. Despite all the pain and bitter disappointment I would not be without that journey for anything in the world. I was different at the end of it. When we left the coach in Paris, I looked at the people and I thought to myself, how naïve I had been at the beginning of that pilgrimage, and it was only a few weeks earlier, when they all looked so holy. To me they looked radiant with the glory of God, and I thought the journey would be one long uninterrupted devotion.

GENEVIEVE: But you learnt pretty soon!

THERESE: I did. We were hardly in the train, and the conversation began. How shocked I was! I felt like thrown off a cliff. These people were Catholics, and the way they spoke! I could not believe it. I had thought that all adults spoke like my dear Papa. And this was only the beginning.

GENEVIEVE: You had your baptism of fire, did you not? Me too.

MOTHER AGNES: But Thérèse is more sensitive. She always was.

GENEVIEVE: I know. What do you think was worst, Thérèse?

THERESE: The priests. The priests of God, and how weak and feeble man is. I knew that I must help them.

(The sun begins to set.)

MOTHER AGNES: You were lucky children, travelling so far, and you could have travelled even further if you had wanted. Papa wanted that – but you were so eager to come and join me? Is that not true?

(Thérèse looks at her but says nothing.)

THERESE: Then it was that Christmas –

GENEVIEVE: *(Gets up and stands behind Thérèse, looking at her painting)*: But it has not got any thorns! Roses have thorns.

THERESE: *(Continues to paint)*: It is not finished. The thorns are coming –

*(Music from Movement 1 starts immediately,
Geneviève looks at Thérèse's painting, then goes back
to her place and continues her own painting.
Light fades to a total blackout. Music continues.)*

MOVEMENT TWO

(Full light comes on to a small study.
Nietzsche is walking up and down. Peter Gast sits writing.)

NIETZSCHE: Can you not write faster? You are so stupid. It is quite incredible.

PETER GAST: I have told you, it is better you give me your manuscripts to copy. This does not work.

NIETZSCHE: Did you buy the leather cover I asked you for?

PETER GAST: Not yet.

NIETZSCHE: Not yet, not yet – can you not say anything else? The fruit, the cloves, have you bought them?

PETER GAST: I have had enough. You use me as your servant: do this, do that. For five weeks I have been doing nothing but attending to you, trying to please you. I have neglected my own work for your sake. – I am not as clever as you, but I am not a fool. Why do you behave like this? It is not only with me. It was the same with Wagner in Bayreuth.

NIETZSCHE: Wagner!

PETER GAST: Yes, Wagner. He was like a father to you at that time, and yet –

NIETZSCHE: You know just as well as I that Wagner is hopeless. He is full of himself.

PETER GAST: I know, but – you must have somebody. And we are all full of ourselves, are we not?

NIETZSCHE: Some have got the right to be "full of themselves".

PETER GAST: Really! Who has got that right?

NIETZSCHE: Why do you ask that question?

PETER GAST: I do not quite know, but – if you are full of yourself, then there is not place for anybody else.

NIETZSCHE: That is precisely the point. That is why the strong super-man must be alone.

PETER GAST: Then Wagner is a super-man.

NIETZSCHE: He thinks he is. That is his problem.

PETER GAST: Is that what it is?

NIETZSCHE: What did you say?

PETER GAST: Nothing. I just muttered to myself.

NIETZSCHE: You do nothing else. And do not dare to speak to me about Wagner again.

PETER GAST: Can your super-man be happy?

NIETZSCHE: What is happiness, Peter?

PETER GAST: To love, and to be loved.

NIETZSCHE: By whom?

PETER GAST: The woman of your heart.

NIETZSCHE: How naïve you are! You do not know woman. You speak like a mediaeval troubadour.

PETER GAST: What's wrong with a troubadour? Wagner too –

NIETZSCHE: Shut up with Wagner!

PETER GAST: But he too has got his Cosima.

NIETZSCHE: Cosima – Once I too wanted to be happy. I wanted to love – But there was not anybody or anything worth loving. Love degrades, Peter. It makes you small. Only the weak, humanity's creepers love. The strong ones fight for power and that brings humanity forward and ennobles it.

PETER GAST: It can also make you a brute.

NIETZSCHE: No, that sort will be extinguished in the struggle toward super-humanity. – But you are too young to understand this, Peter.

PETER GAST: What is super-humanity?

NIETZSCHE: Superman! A grown-up man who stands on his own two feet.

PETER GAST: And woman?

NIETZSCHE: Woman is an animal, for animal purposes.

PETER GAST: Do you say that because that is the only love you have known?

NIETZSCHE: Shut up!

PETER GAST: Is superman happy?

NIETZSCHE: You have asked that question before.

PETER GAST: And you did not answer very well.

NIETZSCHE: I dare say!

PETER GAST: I do not mind what you say, I want to be happy.

NIETZSCHE: Happy! Oh, God you are naïve, can you think of anything else?

PETER GAST: I want to be happy; I want to feel happy and experience love, real love.

NIETZSCHE: Once I wanted that too, but it was not to be. My mission was to be great, to be big. I will be even greater, and then you cannot be "happy". In darkness and emptiness you will be great. It is cold on the top.

PETER GAST: That sounds terrifying.

NIETZSCHE: Greatness is terrifying, Peter, terrifying and lonesome.

PETER GAST: I still think you can be happy.

NIETZSCHE: Then you will be little, a small creep, a worm.

PETER GAST: Must littleness always be degrading?

NIETZSCHE: Yes, and it is disgusting, because it is the bottomscrape of humanity.

PETER GAST: Are we not all little?

NIETZSCHE: You are bcoming obstinate. No! No! We are not all little. You may be. As a matter of fact, let me tell you, you are littler when you try to "stick up" than when you were my little dog. – Everybody longs for a cosy little corner, but there is not any to be found, and the sooner you give up the idea of it the better. Forget it and move on. –

> Tomorrow, and tomorrow and tomorrow,
> Creeps in this petty pace from day to day,
> To the last syllable of recorded time;
> And all our yesterdays have lighted fools
> The way to dusty death. Out, out brief candle!
> Life's but a walking shadow, a poor player
> That struts and frets his hour upon the stage,
> And then is heard no more; it is a tale
> Told by an idiot, full of sound and fury,
> Signifying nothing.

(Short pause.)

PETER GAST: Shakespeare, was it?

NIETZSCHE: Yes.

PETER GAST: Macbeth?

NIETZSCHE *(nods)*: He at least fought for power.

PETER GAST: In a hideous way. And his wife was even worse!

NIETZSCHE: There you see, women are devils.

PETER GAST: They were made, both of them.

NIETZSCHE: Perhaps. But Shakespeare makes them unmask life and the life of it. Life is but a walking shadow, signifying nothing. Can you see that now?

PETER GAST: I suppose so –

NIETZSCHE: That is it, Peter. There is nothing more to it. – Yet I know I have a mission: to tell them that there is nothing – Let us continue.

PETER GAST: All right.

NIETZSCHE: Where was I?

PETER GAST: As when a wanderer who dreams of far distant things –

NIETZSCHE *(Pulls out small pieces of paper from his pocket)*: Suddenly encounters – What did I say?

PETER GAST: Suddenly encounters –

NIETZSCHE: No, no erase that –

PETER GAST: - and leave the rest – ?

NIETZSCHE: Be quiet! – suddenly bumps into – write! Bumps into a sleeping dog in the street *(speaks faster)* a sleeping dog lying in the sun, - just as they then rushed against each other as deadly enemies – these two frightened to death, just so –

PETER GAST: Just a moment, please –

NIETZSCHE: You are a fool! How far did you get?

PETER GAST: Deadly enemies –

NIETZSCHE: Hm, - deadly enemies – frightened to death. Peter, are we deadly enemies?

PETER GAST: Of course not. Whatever has got into you?

NIETZSCHE: I just wondered; to eat or to be eaten. Are you frightened, Peter?

PETER GAST: No, no I am not frightened because I love you. Do you think I would spend all this time with you otherwise?

NIETZSCHE: Peter?

PETER GAST: Yes. – Yes, what is it?

NIETZSCHE: Nothing, nothing really – not at the moment anyway.

PETER GAST: Do you want to continue?

NIETZSCHE: I do not know. I have not decided yet.

PETER GAST: Then if you excuse me, I will go into my room. I have got some letters to write. Call me, when you need me.

NIETZSCHE: This is the limit! Who do you think you are? Caesar? You stay here.

PETER GAST: Not any longer. You have gone too far. You can tighten the string so far, then it breaks. I have done a lot for you, I have slaved for you.

NIETZSCHE: You are a slave and you know it.

PETER GAST: Yes, you despise slaves, yet you need us. If you did not have slaves, you could not be super-man, and what would happen to you then? –

NIETZSCHE: Dusty death. I am a poor player anyway, Peter, on the stage of life.
PETER GAST: Oh my God, how I love you!

NIETZSCHE: Thank you, I need not the love of a slave.

PETER GAST: Yet you need slaves, more than the slave needs you. You cannot tolerate a man equal to yourself.

NIETZSCHE: Are you claiming to be my equal?

PETER GAST: What if I did?

NIETZSCHE: Now this is a new tone. What do you want?

PETER GAST: Some decency.

NIETZSCHE: Am I indecent?

PETER GAST: No, you are not, poor fellow.

NIETZSCHE: Poor fellow! from you! Slaves' rebellion? Go and get my coffee.

PETER GAST: No. This time I say no. I have never said no to you before. I have put up with everything, done everything to please you, but there are limits to what a human being can take.

NIETZSCHE: So you claim humanity, do you? At least that.

PETER GAST: Even at this moment, our last moment together, you can go on like that. Not even a dog can take any amount of kicks. Finally it is enough. It is enough! Everything is finished between us. You will have to get on without me. I cannot take any more, but I will always love you. Goodbye, not Wiedersehen any more, but – Goodbye. *(Exit.)*

NIETZSCHE *(calls after him)*: Peter – I am sorry.

(Curtain. Music.)

(Light onto Thérèse who sits at the window of her cell. She is polishing a silver bowl. After a while the music stops.)

THERESE *(begins to sing, softly at first. Then aloud)*:
> For love of loveliness supreme
> Dying, to cast myself away
> Were bright fulfilment of my dream
> I'd prove my love no easier way; –
> Live, here below, forgotten still,
> A rose before thy path outspread
> At Nazareth; or on Calvary's hill
> Relieve thy last, thy labouring tread.

(Sometimes she coughs. Then a fierce coughing attack. She coughs into her handkerchief. After the attack she looks at the handkerchief, that is stained with blood. She looks for a while at the blood, then smiles.)

THERESE: Blood! – blood. Oh, my God, I am really coming to you. I am sick – I will come to you. Oh my –

(Another coughing attack interrupts her. After the attack there is more blood on the handkerchief. Thérèse looks at it, folds it slowly.)

THERESE: I am going to heaven. I am so happy! I will see God, all the angels, the Blessed Virgin and I will meet my Mama again, my sisters and brothers – and my Papa – Oh, my Papa! – Your little queen

is coming to you now, soon – soon – In heaven we will dance and sing.
We will play, we will all play together and be so happy. I am going
to play the violin, oh! oh! *(claps her hands)* My God, my God, Jesus,
Mother – Mother *(Pause; stares in front of her)* Mother! – Mother!
– For there is a heaven, is there not? Tell me, tell me! Yes, of course
there is a heaven. – God – God! You are waiting for me, are you not?
Answer! Answer me! Why are you so silent? – The blood. The blood
is real. It is real. It must mean something. – Blood is life. It is life.
When it is gone, there is no more life, no more life – life. But I want
to live, I want to live. Do you understand, I want to live! Do you hear
me? I want to live, live! I cannot die, I cannot die now, I am too young.
– Oh God, I have not lived yet, I have not even begun to live. – Jesus,
you were at least thirty when they crucified you, but I am only twenty.
Hold my hand, please, hold my hand. I am so frightened and so little. I
cannot manage, I cannot manage this. Why do you ask so much? You,
you – if you are there at all – Oh God –
If this is the end, then it must continue. It must go on, it cannot be
finished. The sun must rise again on the other side of the mountains.
It will shine, it will shine and the sky will be blue again and I will
pick fresh roses. I will pick all the buds. – Perhaps it is all a dream – a
dream – *(violent coughing-attack, more blood on the handkerchief)*
– It is real. It is true. This is the end.
Oh God – God –
Good blessed Virgin, help me, help me –

(Music. Curtain.)

MOVEMENT THREE

(The whole scene takes place in the darkness.)
(Knocking on the door.)

THERESE: Mother, Mother open! Open please, open! Let me in! *(Knocking)* Mother help! –

(Quick light steps; knocking.)

THERESE: Open! Open, please! Help! *(Knocking.)* *(Knocking.)*
(Pause)
(Light steps; knocking.)

THERESE: Open! Open, please! Open *(Knocking.)* Open to me, help! Help me! *(Knocking.)*
(Knocking, quick steps, knocking.)
(Pause.) *(Knocking.)*

THERESE: Please open! Open the door! Open! I want to see a priest!
(Knocking.)
(Short pause.)

THERESE: Why is nobody available?
(Pause.)

(Full light on Thérèse, wrapped up in blankets, in the same garden as in Movement One. It is autumn. Sr Geneviève is gently shaking Thérèse whose book and pen have fallen to the ground.)

25

SR GENEVIEVE: Wake up Thérèse, wake up!

THERESE: Oh, oh! – Where am I – Oh –

SR GENEVIEVE: Are you all right now?

THERESE: Yes, I am fine now. I think I fell asleep.

SR GENEVIEVE: Yes, you did. You dropped your book too. *(Picks it up.)* Are you sure you will be all right now?

THERESE: Yes, thank you my dear, my dear sister. What should I do without you? *(Begins to write. Sr Geneviève kisses her on the forehead and leaves the stage. Thérèse continues to write.)*

THERESE *(without looking up)*: The story of a soul *(continues to write for a while, then stops.)* I never knew – I never knew, how could I? The watchmaker's little daughter – Papa's little queen. How could I have known that it was possible, – such darkness – such loneliness – such emptiness and cold. How can it be possible? All the thoughts that pass through my mind – I do not want them. If the sisters knew these thoughts they would throw me out of the house. – Only when you have been through it, do you know. – Not even death is a relief, for – what then? Oh, no –
My God, I do not ask for relief. I say Yes to everything, accept everything for love of You, even the most extravagant thoughts that come into my mind.

*(She sits still for a while then continues to write,
looks up at the sky. An old nun enters the stage.)*

OLD NUN: It is beautiful. – And soon you will be there. Just imagine, soon you will be in heaven. Soon you will be with all your loved ones again; with our Lady and all the angels and saints. – You must remember us then, when you are up there with God, and so happy, so happy. How happy you are!

(Thérèse smiles but does not answer. The old nun walks away.)

THERESE: Dear old Sr Martina, if she but knew! If she could read my soul, she would be amazed and horrified. If she knew I was only admiring the material sky in its beauty; the other heaven remains closed to me. – Oh, my God! It is so dark, so dark – I never knew it was possible to doubt – the chill of the night, the darkness, the cold – emptiness, just emptiness – no consolation, no reassurance – My God! Are you there? Why are you so silent? Are you there at all? Or is there nothing? –
I must stop. Otherwise I might blaspheme. – All is darkness – and the fear that I am going to a greater darkness, – total annihilation. Oh, God help me! The iron-grip round my heart that has not slackened one minute for eighteen months – and those months have been like centuries – so long, so long – day after day, week after week in an endless chain – Nevertheless my God, I do not ask you to take this from me and to lift the darkness, only that I do not offend you. But I offer this for all sinners and unbelievers; now that I can sit at table with them – one of them – now I know what it is like. – It is so hard – Oh good Blessed Virgin, come to my aid – help us all. Help us unbelievers. Help us to believe! – To believe! – believe!!
Never must they leave poison or strong medicine next to a very sick person. If they but knew; the temptation to finish it all – I know, I know –

(After a while Mother Gonzague and a well-dressed gentleman in his forties enter the stage. Thérèse does not notice them coming.)

DOCTOR: How is she doing?

MOTHER GONZAGUE: It is up and down; sometimes better, sometimes worse. These last two days she has been comparatively well, even being able to eat a little.

DOCTOR: How are you today, Sister?

THERESE *(looking up)*: I am fine, thanks; just tired.

DOCTOR: Lazy bones? Let me check you pulse.

MOTHER GONZAGUE: Would you like us to go inside to the infirmary, so that you can examine her? We do not usually see the doctor in the garden.

DOCTOR: There is always a first time, Mother. No, we do not need to go inside. I am not going to examine her. I was just passing by and thought I would drop in and see how she was getting on.

(He takes her wrist, frowns as he takes her pulse, but says nothing. Thérèse looks at him anxiously.)

DOCTOR *(looks up seriously)*: I also brought two pills for you to try. If you find them helpful, we can order them from Paris. It is a new pill, rather expensive, but so far it has proved very helpful. It will not cure you, but it will ease the breathing a lot and you will be much more comfortable.

THERESE: Thank you doctor, I –

MOTHER GONZAGUE: We do not seek comfort, doctor.

(Thérèse looks helplessly at the doctor.)

DOCTOR: Well, forget the world if you do not like it, but try the pill and see if it helps.

THERESE *(looks at Mother Gonzague shyly)*: Shall we?

DOCTOR: You are the patient, and you follow my instructions. *(Turns to Mother Gonzague.)* Give her one a day; in the morning.

MOTHER GONZAGUE: Yes, doctor.

THERESE *(looks at the doctor)*: Is there no chance? Is it certain I will die?

DOCTOR: I am afraid so.

THERESE: How long – ?

DOCTOR *(shrugs his shoulders)*: It can be a week. The sickness has reached a very advanced state. – But you could also linger for months.

MOTHER GONZAGUE: Well, my child. You will go to heaven. It is waiting for you. You are lucky.

DOCTOR: Would you like to change roles?

THERESE *(turns to the doctor)*: Do you believe in Heaven?

DOCTOR: No.

(Mother Gonzague gasps for breath.)

THERESE *(intensely looking at the doctor)*: Why?

DOCTOR: Because I do not believe in God.

> *(Mother Gonzague sighs and opens her mouth*
> *to say something, but Thérèse speaks first.)*

THERESE: Are you sure there is no God?

DOCTOR: Yes, I cannot see any point in speculating about metaphysics. It is quite enough to look after what we have here.

MOTHER GONZAGUE: Monsieur Legrange, we did not know, hm, that you were a, hm, a free-thinker.

DOCTOR: Would you not have consulted me then?

MOTHER GONZAGUE: We had only heard that you were the best lung-specialist in France.

DOCTOR: And now? Do you still think so?

THERESE: Doctor, we are very grateful for all that you are doing for me *(Mother Gonzague looks at her. Thérèse adds emphatically.)* I am. – If you do not believe in God, what about us human beings?

DOCTOR: I believe in humanity, yes.

THERESE: But man must be created by God – *(looking intensely at the doctor.)*

DOCTOR: The human race is just another species that has developed on the earth along with the other animals.

MOTHER GONZAGUE: This is going too far. You are upsetting the patient.

DOCTOR *(smiles)*: I do not think so. The patients never ask more than they are prepared to hear. And it is very bad to leave them with their questions unanswered.

THERESE: But what about the questions that have no answers?

DOCTOR: There are no such questions. We may not have the answers today, but future development will solve the problems.

MOTHER GONZAGUE *(directly to Thérèse)*: You will know everything in Heaven.

(Thérèse looks bewildered at the two.)

DOCTOR: I must go. Look after yourself Sister. *(Turns to Mother Gonzague)* Take good care of her. I will be back, if not tomorrow, the next day.

THERESE: Thank you, doctor. What have you got in your pocket?

DOCTOR: A book.

THERESE: May I have a look?

DOCTOR: It is not a book for you.

THERESE: How do you know?

DOCTOR: I am sure, Mother would not approve of this book.

MOTHER GONZAGUE: I am sure too.

DOCTOR: There you see, Sister.

THERESE: What is it called?

DOCTOR: It is a German book, called *Also sprach Zarathustra.*

THERESE: What does that mean?

DOCTOR: Thus spoke Zarathustra.

THERESE: What does he say?

DOCTOR: Mother would be very angry with me if I told you that.

MOTHER GONZAGUE: We only read good books.

DOCTOR: I am sure.

THERESE: Please, do tell me what it is all about.

MOTHER GONZAGUE: Sister, this is enough.

THERESE: Who is Zarathustra?

DOCTOR: Another time – perhaps.

MOTHER GONZAGUE: No other time.

DOCTOR: Goodbye, Sister, see you soon.

THERESE: Goodbye, Doctor.

> *(The doctor and Mother Gonzague leave the stage.*
> *Thérèse looks after them.)*

MOTHER GONZAGUE: She is very sick.

DOCTOR: I know that.

MOTHER GONZAGUE: That is why she talks so much nonsense.

DOCTOR: Is it nonsense?

THERESE *(looking after them in silence for a while)*: And he is such a good man – doing so much good – *(she shakes her head, – music – begins to write.)* Oh good Jesus, never did I think one could suffer so much. – I no longer believe in death for me, I believe only in suffering – so much the better. – My God, My God, why have you deserted me?

> *(Music from Movement Three; Thérèse remains immoveable*
> *in full light for a while. Then total blackout. Music continues.)*

*(Light comes on, music stops. Nietzsche is writing at
his desk in the same study as in Movement Two.
The room is considerably emptier now.)*

A MAID *(enters and hands him a letter)*: A letter, Sir.

NIETZSCHE: Thanks. *(Opens the letter as the maid leaves the room.)*
Hm – from Overbeck – faithful old Overbeck. He is the only real friend
I have ever had. – Yes, Peter Gast too in his own little way, that is true.
There were others *(he looks up)* but they faded away; the friendship, if
such it was, died, quietly and unconspicuously or violently. *(Then he
begins to read the letter. As he reads he takes out a small photo that
was enclosed in the letter. Nietzsche reads in silence, then)* Yesterday,
the family went for an outing to the woods, near the little lake you
know so well. The weather was beautiful *(Nietzsche reads in silence
then picks up the photo, looks at it.)* The little fellow looks just like his
father. Overbeck is lucky. He will live on in his children. The species
will continue. When I go there will be nothing – absolutely nothing.
Nothing left – but my writing. My writing will live on. It belongs to
posterity. I know that. Some people are born posthumously. We are
too great for our time. – Perhaps that is why I am so lonely – must be
– so alone. *(Reads in silence; then aloud.)* Hope you are well and not
working too hard. Ida sends her regards. *(Reads the rest in silence.)*
They all have their families. I alone am left, left all alone. Perhaps it
had to be so. I was called, – was I? – called to be Zarathustra; all alone
on the high mountain peak, calling out, declaring, proclaiming the
destiny – the destiny of whom? – It is lonesome and cold up on the top.
It is warmer further down, with the crowd. But, I am rather alone and
cold, than warm and cosy with the burgeois in their petty little corner.
– The price must be paid.
(After a while.) There was a time when I too longed for the ordinary,

the homely, the little pastoral, I looked for a wife.

– I reallly loved Lou. Yes, I loved her, as I have never loved a woman. That time it was not only the animal. It was more to it than that, – but she – the monkey – traitor! Woman, a mistake of nature! She should be whipped! *(Picks up the letter,)* I must answer this straight away. The post from here takes a long time. And Overbeck deserves an answer. Thank you for your letter. A letter from you is always a joy, but also pain. It reminds me of how lonely I am. I literally have nobody. I have neither wife nor God. So there is no meaning for me, no purpose either here or hereafter, the non-existing here-after. At least I have got the courage to face that. Many people today boldly and loudly proclaim they have no religious belief and yet they continue to act and behave as if there were a "higher authority" to direct and order their lives. They have not got the courage to take the consequences of the death of God. Perhaps the next century will do so. Dostojevsky was right; "If God does not exist, everything is permissible". That is so, my friend. That is why I stand firm and hold on to the moral nihilism that is but a logical consequence of the total collapse of metaphysics. Forgive me for being so philosophical. I know you put up with me. When nobody else does you do. *(Crosses out.)* What else is there anyway?

Hypocrisy, nothing else, do you not agree? I know you do, but do not say that to Ida. She would be upset if she knew what I told you. Greet her from me, please. *(Writes in silence for a while.)* But it is hard to be homeless. Somehow I always had the feeling I was – and had to be homeless. Already as a young lad I sensed it when I wrote "Homeless". Do you remember?

> Fleet horses bear me,
> Without fear or dismay,
> Through distant places.
> And whoever sees me knows me,

and whoever knows me calls me:
The homeless man –

No one dares
To ask me
Where my home is:
Perhaps I have never been fettered
To space and the flying hours,
Am as free as an eagle! –

(Short pause, then he continues to write.) However, I am sure I have got something to say, a message. Even if I am not hearkened to today, I will be tomorrow. I am a man of the future. If I were not sure of this I would not go on living – I would not live. I am convinced I have a mission; otherwise I would have finished it off long ago. *(Music, Nietzsche continues to write, light fades. Thérèse enters, sits down unnoticed.)* Superman – but I am afraid. If Peter saw me now? – I am so afraid.

THERESE: Let us be afraid together.

NIETZSCHE: Who are you?

THERESE: A friend.

NIETZSCHE: I do not think we have met.

THERESE: We are friends, you know that, do you not?

NIETZSCHE: What do you want?

THERESE: To ask you a question.

NIETZSCHE: Ask then, milady.

THERESE: Thank you.

NIETZSCHE: I did not say I would answer you.

THERESE: You will.

NIETZSCHE: Are you sure?

THERESE: I am.

NIETZSCHE: I did not say I would answer you.

THERESE: You will.

NIETZSCHE: Are you sure?

THERESE: I am.

NIETZSCHE: I dare say, you are a little madam.

THERESE: Do you think so.

NIETZSCHE: Nice! Now, ask your question, if you want.

THERESE: Where is your home?

NIETZSCHE *(stares at her)*: How long have you been here?

THERESE: I have just come.

NIETZSCHE: You lie.

THERESE: I never lie.

NIETZSCHE: Ha! Is there anything else you want?

THERESE: Come with me.

NIETZSCHE: To where?

THERESE: Just come with me.

NIETZSCHE: I will not come, unless you tell me where we are going.

THERESE: Come please!

NIETZSCHE: To where? For the last time, where are we going?

THERESE: I do not know.

NIETZSCHE: You are a good one! What are we going to do then?

THERESE: Just come with me, please. Please, come.

NIETZSCHE: What do you really want?

THERESE: I just want you to come with me.

NIETZSCHE: And do you think it is too much that I want to know what we are going to do?

THERESE: I suppose not.

NIETZSCHE: I suppose! It is my time to ask now, and you answer. Is it too much or not?

THERESE: I, I do not really know.

NIETZSCHE: I do not really know!!

THERESE: I cannot answer. I cannot answer all these questions, but please, come. Please come with me, just come.

NIETZSCHE: Is that what you are out after? I suspected that.

THERESE: Why do you make everything ugly?

NIETZSCHE: Life is ugly.

THERESE: It is beautiful too.

NIETZSCHE: Then it is soft. The strong is ugly, or at least it looks ugly to the weak.

THERESE: Why must you be ugly to be strong?

NIETZSCHE: Do not trouble yourself, it is too much for your little head.

THERESE: I want to know why beautiful cannot be strong.

NIETZSCHE: You ask too many questions.

THERESE: I always have.

NIETZSCHE: Hm –

THERESE: Are you coming or not.

NIETZSCHE: For the last time, to do what?

THERESE: Walk.

NIETZSCHE: Walk, to where?

THERESE: To freedom.

NIETZSCHE: What does a woman like you know about freedom? Women are for slavery.

THERESE: You do not mean that, do you?

NIETZSCHE: Why not?

THERESE: And who is free then?

NIETZSCHE: Those who have power.

THERESE: We will all have power.

NIETZSCHE: Impossible!

THERESE: Why can we not share power?

NIETZSCHE: I am not discussing the topic any further with a woman, especially somebody as young as you. Women are made to be slaves.

THERESE: That sounds terrible.

NIETZSCHE: Just too bad if it does.

THERESE: You frighten me.

NIETZSCHE: That might make you think. –

THERESE: I am sure I am free – or will be.

NIETZSCHE: Free to fall into the abyss.

THERESE: I know. I know that. Can we not be afraid together? Please.

NIETZSCHE: I am not afraid.

THERESE: Of course you are.

NIETZSCHE: I am not.

THERESE: Can we not be afraid together, and walk together?

NIETZSCHE: To where?

THERESE: To freedom.

NIETZSCHE: And fall into the abyss?

THERESE: Let us fall together.

NIETZSCHE: You fall alone.

THERESE: But we must help each other.

NIETZSCHE: You fall alone and there is no help.

THERESE: There is help.

NIETZSCHE: You will see that there is not. There is nothing there.

THERESE: Do not frighten me so.

NIETZSCHE: So you are afraid?

THERESE: Of course I am. That is why I know that you are afraid too. Let us be together.

NIETZSCHE: I do not need you.

THERESE: But I need you.

NIETZSCHE: Really?

THERESE: Yes. Come, please come.

NIETZSCHE: Are you not afraid of me?

THERESE: Me? Why should I be afraid of you?

NIETZSCHE: I might kill you.

THERESE: No, you will not. You would not kill a horse. – Why do you say these things?

NIETZSCHE: I do not really know.

THERESE: You are right, you do not.

NIETZSCHE: Forget that! I was thinking of something else. You distract me.

THERESE: I am sorry, but why do you want to hurt? You do not really, do you?

NIETZSCHE: We must hurt, because the fight for survival is the progress of humanity.

THERESE: What about all the little ones?

NIETZSCHE: They will be extinguished.

THERESE: That is horrible! I cannot believe that you mean what you are saying.

NIETZSCHE: So it is, if you like it or not.

THERESE: Then, many people will just disappear; those who cannot fight, the weak, the sick. And what about those who lose the battle?

NIETZSCHE: They will go the same way.

THERESE: Oh, my God! – Poor you, poor you.

NIETZSCHE: I am not poor, and I do not need your compassion. Thank you.

THERESE: You do need me, and I will come back.

NIETZSCHE: You are not coming back.

THERESE: I am. I promise you, I will come back.

NIETZSCHE: I know what a woman's promise is worth.

THERESE: Poor you.

NIETZSCHE: Stop that.

THERESE: Please, let us walk together.

NIETZSCHE: We had better part.

THERESE: Why?

NIETZSCHE: We are too different.

THERESE: That does not matter.

NIETZSCHE: We do not fit together.

THERESE: We can, we can try.

NIETZSCHE: No, we must part.

THERESE *(gets up slowly)*: I will come back.

NIETZSCHE: You will not.

THERESE: I promise you, I will.

NIETZSCHE: Women never keep their promises.

THERESE: I do. *(Disappears discreetly, more light.)*

(Curtain.)

MOVEMENT FOUR

(Music stops and full light onto Thérèse,
lying in bed in the infirmary, reading her Bible.)

THERESE: When I came to you, it was not with any show of oratory and philosophy – the only knowledge I claimed to have was about Jesus, and only about Him as the crucified Christ. – My vocation is love. To be love. – To be love in the heart of the Church, my Mother. It was the great Apostle that taught me that – But love that costs. – A chalice of love and suffering – to be emptied – all alone in the night.

(Sr Geneviève enters with some fresh roses in a vase. She puts the vase down on the table next to Thérèse's bed.)

GENEVIEVE: I brought you some roses.

THERESE: Thanks.

(Sr Geneviève arranges the roses. Thérèse looks at her.)

THERESE *(softly)*: Are you afraid to die?

GENEVIEVE *(without taking her eyes from the roses)*: I suppose I am – I have not thought about it. – Are you?

THERESE: You know, it is strange, when you are there and it is your turn, it is different – it is like not real and yet – more real – it is as if it were so deep so it cannot be fathomed – but you must throw yourself

47

– throw yourself head-long into it, trusting that He is there and that He is holding you. *(The two sisters look at each other but say nothing.)* To die is different from being dead. There are many dead, but you, you alone die your own death. That is what is so frightening.

GENEVIEVE: You talk like a philosopher.

THERESE: Perhaps I am one, old and wise, yes, I am old now, you smile, but you see, you are always old when you die. Your age does not matter. God makes you old. The fruit must ripen and then fall. It can fall a long, long way and hurt itself when it hits the ground, but it must fall, otherwise it will rot on the tree and not be of any use. You must chose to fall *(she nods her head.)* – When I knew that I was old enough to be little, to be a little child with God as my Father. In darkness and pain He is my father – a very silent Father – I keep telling myself that again and again. Do you believe that? He loves so much, and He demands so much. We too must love, Céline, we must love very much. Oh, Céline, how much we must love. We must love until it hurts – and it hurts very much. – Love must crush us to nothingness, then we will live.

GENEVIEVE: Where?

THERESE: On a cross.

GENEVIEVE: But you cannot live on a cross!

THERESE: You cannot live anywhere else. There is not anything else. – Pray that I die there.

GENEVIEVE: I will. *(Fiddles with the roses.)*

THERESE: Nobody tells us anything from the other side. We can only talk about the bridge when we are crossing it. – My God – do not let the bridge collapse, do not let it fall into the abyss –

GENEVIEVE: I do not quite understand, Thérèse. What is all that about bridges and abysses.

THERESE: Never mind, Céline, I love you. You know that, do you not?

GENEVIEVE: I know, and I love you too. When you are up there, you will not forget me, will you?

THERESE: No – *(there is an awkward silence.)* – When I have gone, you must teach my little way. You must tell the little ones that they are great, and the great that they are little. That will be the difficult thing. We are all little. That is so good, and so hard. You know it is hard to let God take the rein, because He does not tell you where He is driving. You just have to go along with Him, and He does not tell you anything. You must just trust Him, and He tests you to the utmost. Many times He leaves you in the dark or in an empty deserted place without a word. You have no idea if you will ever find Him again. Oh, Céline, if you knew what it is like – You must be big to know you are little. The little way is not an easy way out, or the road of a spoilt child. – I was spoilt once, that is true, but I have grown up. Only when I had grown up, did I know what it is to be a child. Do you understand?

GENEVIEVE: Not quite.

THERESE: You must be strong and you are strong when you know you are weak. When you think you are strong, you are weak. When you think you are strong you are weak. If you are not afraid you cannot be brave.

(Here a coughing attack interrupts her flow of words.)

GENEVIEVE: Poor Thérèse. Can I help you?

THERESE: I know how hard it is – how dark, how narrow the road – with precipices on both sides – the abyss, the abyss of darkness calling you, drawing you, even pulling you downwards. – No wonder the priest warned me of eternal damnation. – Staggering along the Little Way is not easy. – Now I know why so many let go into the abyss. *(Puts her left hand in front of her forehead.)* I wanted to suffer and I have been heard. I have suffered very much. – One morning, during my act of thanksgiving after Communion, I felt the agony of death – and with it no consolation. Oh, Céline, it was, it was terrible! I was so frightened.

MOTHER GONZAGUE *(Enters)*: I did not know Sister was here.

THERESE: But, - Mother, you have given her leave –

MOTHER GONZAGUE: Yes, I know.

THERESE: She brought me some flowers. Are they not pretty?

MOTHER GONZAGUE *(Looks at the flowers)*: Very pretty.

THERESE: But they have thorns. Roses have thorns.

MOTHER GONZAGUE: They usually do. How are you today, my child?

THERESE: It is only suffering now, Mother – no consolation, no relief. – You must help me, you must help me to die.

MOTHER GONZAGUE: Poor child. – I came to ask you to continue to write your autobiography. You can manage that, can you not?

THERESE: Yes, Mother. – I just write what comes to the pen. I do not worry about it.

(Mother Agnes enters. Mother Gonzague stiffens.)

MOTHER GONZAGUE: I see this is going to be a family gathering. Well, I had better leave the Martin daughters to enjoy themselves. *(Walks out.)*

THERESE and MOTHER AGNES: Mother.

MOTHER AGNES: Oh, she is difficult.

THERESE: It is not easy for her.

GENEVIEVE *(to Mother Agnès)*: Why must you two always fight?

MOTHER AGNES: You must not talk like that, Céline.

GENEVIEVE: But it is true.

THERESE: Pray, pray Céline, pray much.

GENEVIEVE: I still want to know why.

MOTHER AGNES: There are certain things that one must not ask about.

GENEVIEVE: That is not right. It has been like this all the time. I am not going to put up with it.

THERESE: There are some things that you must suffer in silence. When your hands are tied and you cannot help although you want to. You learn, but it is hard. Injustice is hard, more so when it hits the one you love.

GENEVIEVE: Then something must be done.

THERESE: And what are you going to do about it?

GENEVIEVE: I do not know.

THERESE: There you see. There comes a time when you can just be there and suffer. Another Mary on Calvary.

GENEVIEVE: I am not Mary and I am not going to keep silent. It is plain jealousy, that is what it is, nothing but jealousy.

MOTHER AGNES: Hush, do not talk like that.

GENEVIEVE: Hush, hush, I am tired of this secrecy. Why can we not call things by their right names? If it is jealousy call it jealousy.

MOTHER AGNES: Everything must not be spoken out, that just is not the done thing.

GENEVIEVE: I am not going to put up with everything and keep quiet. I am not an angel.

THERESE: We should really be like angels.

GENEVIEVE: You must always say something pious. Oh, yes, angels and then we will fight who are going to be the seraphim and cherubim.

MOTHER AGNES: Children, children, you must not argue. We must not upset Thérèse.

THERESE: I am not upset.

GENEVIEVE: She knows more about it than you think.

MOTHER AGNES: I am sure. Pray for us, Thérèse. Come, Céline, we must go now and leave our little angel to rest.

GENEVIEVE: At least somebody is an angel.

(Exit Mother Agnes and Geneviève.)

THERESE: If there are any angels – Oh, my God.

(Music. Light fades to a total blackout.)

*(Curtain opens, Thérèse is in bed. Mother Gonzague and
the Doctor enter, talking quietly to each other.)*

DOCTOR: And how have you been behaving since I last saw you?

(Mother Gonzague looks at Thérèse.)

THERESE: Pretty much the same. I cannot die, I cannot live. *(She makes a grimace, looks at the doctor with a little smile.)*

(Sr Geneviève enters, walks up to Mother Gonzague and whispers something.)

MOTHER GONZAGUE: Tell him to wait. I will come. *(Sr Geneviève leaves the room.)* I am afraid I have to go and attend to some urgent business. I will be back in a few minutes. *(Leaves the room.)*

THERESE: I have been waiting for you to come back and I have been dreading it.

DOCTOR: Why?

THERESE: You challenge me. – My long fought-for peace, always fragile, always brittle, is challenged by your unbelief. Why do you not believe in God?

DOCTOR: Why do you believe?

THERESE: When I entered the convent – well, actually all the time until I got sick. I would have thought you were mad, asking such a question. Some would have said you were wicked, like a wicked beast, but – somehow I never believed that. I could never believe that, not even as a child, that anybody was really wicked, deep inside. I could not explain it – I still really cannot – but – no *(they look at each other)* – people can be mistaken, sinful, proud, but deep, deep down there is a good little child in everybody.

Yes, *(abruptly)* I knew you would laugh at me.

DOCTOR: I am not laughing. A smile is not laughter. You have still got a long way to go, sister, if you do not know the difference between a smile and laughter. And I was not sarcastic. You are just so different, so different from the people I know. Mind you, I do not know many nuns, but – you seem pretty different from those I see here too. Go on, sister, I want to hear more.

THERESE: It was my upbringing, too, of course: happy, sheltered, perhaps too much so. You would say narrow – well, we have not got a choice, have we? But, I was happy. Of course there were the ordinary ups and downs of life. I was a sickly child. *(Doctor listens intently.)* And you must remember my mother died when I was still little. Then my father's illness; that was terrible, the shame, the humiliation. That my father should have to suffer so. It was like seeing God suffer. My poor Papa.

DOCTOR: What was it?

THERESE: I do not know exactly, but it was something mental. – Apart from that I was basically happy and at peace, until – until the darkness, total darkness descended. –
(Turns to the Doctor.) That is why – if you had asked that question about faith a few months ago, I think I would have committed suicide. –

But I have fought through the darkness now. It is still dark, complete darkness, but I can rest in the dark. But do not shake me. It still hurts. *(Shakes her head, looks at the doctor with a mischievious smile.)* You do not understand this, do you? –

DOCTOR: Yes and no. But I want you to tell me more about it.

THERESE: In our home, God was taken for granted. He was a given in life, like your parents. *(She is silent for a while, fiddles with the blanket.)*

DOCTOR*(mumbles)*: A simple, easy world, where the sun always shines.

THERESE: Not much of interest happened in my life. Yes, there was the pilgrimage to Rome, that was an eye-opener in many ways, too short perhaps. But I met many different people, all kinds of people that I would never have known otherwise. A little peep into the big world.

DOCTOR: Big, bad world?

THERESE: I do not know, I suppose so. – Then I came here. Two of my older sisters were here already, so in a way it was like coming home. *(He smiles.)* It was not all a sweet idyll. You must not think that. Life in a convent is not easy.

DOCTOR: I can imagine that.

THERESE: And there were several sisters who were very displeased to have three blood-sisters in the same community – and when Céline came! That was anything but popular! In fact I never thought she would be allowed to enter.

DOCTOR: So there are four of you in the house!

THERESE: And a cousin!!

DOCTOR: Have I met any of them?

THERESE: The one who came just now with a message for mother; that was Sr Geneviève, that is Céline's religious name.

DOCTOR: Why do you change your names when you become nuns?

THERESE: I do not know, but they have always done that. It is an old tradition.

DOCTOR: Does that not make you lose your identity, your touch with reality? Or is that what they want?

THERESE: I do not think so. It is not always done. My name was not changed. My patron saint has always been the great foundress of our order, St Teresa of Avila. You should read her. She is a woman you would like, I am sure. She was a great mystic and a woman with her feet firmly on the ground. She had not lost touch with reality. And she had a great wit. You would not leave her with the answer.

DOCTOR: If you lend me one of her books, I promise to read it. How old were you when you entered the convent?

THERESE: Fifteen.

DOCTOR: Fifteen! God help us! You were still a child. But – I mean – It is ridiculous! How can anybody mature in these circumstances, in such a closed up – and excuse me for being blunt, narrow environment?

THERESE: There was a lot of criticism and a lot of talk about it in town at the time.

(Stage moves to her 'memory'.)

(This scene is optional; producer's choice).
(Two ladies come walking along the street in
a small nineteenth century town.)

MME A: I believe the youngest of the Martin daughters is entering the convent too.

MME B *(stops horrified)*: Never! She is just a child!

MMEA: Nevertheless – All the permissions have been granted. She is entering next week.

MME B: But it is ludicrous! She will never grow up. I do not think she even had an ordinary schooling.

MME A: No, it is a strange family; very pious and good – but – some-how peculiar.

MME B: Religious fanatics, I think.

MME A: If there are gentle fanatics, yes!

MME B: What do you mean.

MME A: I do not really know. But, – they are very quiet, discreet people. They would not disturb anybody.

MME B: This is the point: they are unreal. Monsieur Guerin, the pharmacist, with all his militant religion, is much more real. These old fighters are flesh and blood people anyway. You feel at home with them. He was Madame Martin's brother, you know.

MME A: Really! I did not know that. I would hardly have believed it. But of course, he is an educated man –

MME B: Yes, these are strange times we live in – some people so pious and religious so you do not know if they are a little insane or just romantic dreamers, and others do not believe at all and seem to rejoice in blaspheming. In the end you do not know what to believe yourself.

MME A: I certainly know what I believe – but it is frightening. – Nobody knows what is right and wrong any longer.

(They continue to walk in silence.)

MME B *(stops and looks at something off stage.)*: Look, is that not Madame Pitot, pruning her roses?

MME A: Oh, yes, so it is. She is always pruning her roses. And she is hard on them. *(Gasps.)* Oh, look! She is rough, is she not?

MME B: She knows how to do it. You must be hard at the pruning if you want to have really beautiful roses. The harder the pruning the more perfect the rose.

MME A: Yes, I know. And she certainly has a magnificent rose garden. – She is cutting some now.

MME B: Oh, yes – she is. Hm. Strange way she cuts; some almost finished, some in their prime and some only buds – Peculiar –

MME A: I like roses. It is just a pity they have so many thorns.

MME B: And they say that the most beautiful roses have the sharpest thorns –

MME A: I wonder if that is true –
(They walk in silence, and the light fades.)

(Back to Thérèse and the Doctor in the infirmary.)
(END OF OPTIONAL SCENE.)

(Doctor and Thérèse sit silent for a while.)

THERESE: Do you think I am immature?

DOCTOR: No, I do not actually – and that surprises me. That is why I would like to know more about you.

THERESE: I was amused at you just now; when you were so horrified at my early entry into Carmel, you said: God help us! I have heard that before: atheists and agnostics – and if you knew how I feel one with you – calling on the God they say they do not believe in.

DOCTOR: That is just a habitual expression.

THERESE: And where does the habit come from?

DOCTOR: I suppose childhood superstition.

THERESE: Are you sure it is superstition?

DOCTOR: What else could it be?

THERESE: If it were true?

DOCTOR: I do not think so, Sister. Life is not a fairytale, "where they live happily ever after", –

THERESE: Do you remember I said that if you had asked me these questions about faith a few months ago I would have committed suicide and if you had asked them when I entered I would have thought you were mad. Today I do neither –
If I try to describe to you what has happened to me, something I do not quite understand myself, much less can I explain it, then you will see how I have grown up, from a naïve child to an old woman. Now I can see that I was very much a child, and very much the youngest child in the family, when I entered here – Even if I were not stupid, I was very inexperienced. – But it is as if I had had a whole long life. And now it is over. It was long, very long, but short too. – Does this make sense to you, or do you think I am mad? Sometimes I wonder if I am mad after all – when those strange wild thoughts come. I do not even know from where. Then I wish I could be like the other sisters. It would be so much easier.

DOCTOR: Would you really like that?

THERESE: No, I would not, that is why it is so strange. I would not want to be without all this. I cannot think of life without the darkness now. The darkness is God's gift to me. Yet I am afraid, I am so frightened. – Do you understand? –

Now it is only to fall, so easy and so difficult. I must fall, like a fruit or a flower. – Sometimes I want to and sometimes I do not. I am both young and old, it is so strange.

DOCTOR *(softly)*:
    Sweet rose, fair flower, untimely pluck'd, soon faded,
    Pluck'd in the bud, and faded in the spring!
    Bright orient pearl, alack! too timely shaded;
    Fair creature, kill'd too soon by death's sharp string!
    Like a green plum that hangs upon a tree.
    And falls, through wind, before the fall should be.

THERESE: What are you saying?

DOCTOR: I just remembered some lines from school.

THERESE: It sounded like poetry.

DOCTOR: It was Shakespeare.

THERESE: Oh. – Do you like literature? *(He shrugs his shoulders.)* I do. I wish I had had a whole life to read and study.

DOCTOR: Literature is like religion, just fiction.

THERESE: Do you believe that anything is real?

DOCTOR: The physical world around us is real enough.

THERESE: But surely there must be more to it than that. – What about beauty? – Goodness –

(Music)

What about music?

DOCTOR: It is all right.

THERESE: But do you like it?

DOCTOR: Some music, yes.

THERESE: What music do you like?

DOCTOR: Different sorts.

THERESE: I like violin. I would like to play the violin.

DOCTOR: I prefer organ music.

THERESE: That is Church music!

DOCTOR: That does not matter. Music is music.

THERESE: But it speaks about something.

DOCTOR: I suppose it does.

THERESE: You think it is beautiful, do you not?

DOCTOR: You are determined to make me say "beautiful", are you not?

THERESE: Hm. –

DOCTOR: I think you are a beautiful young woman.

THERESE: Not now. I am old and haggard. *(A coughing attack inter-rupts her.)*

DOCTOR *(looks gently and searchingly at Thérèse)*: Try to relax and just let the cough come.

(After the attack Thérèse tries to speak.)

DOCTOR: No, not yet; wait a little.

(They remain silent.)

THERESE: Nobody seems to understand, when I say I am old, least of all my own sisters. I grew up very fast, too fast perhaps. It is painful to grow, and the faster you grow the more painful it is, and the pain remains. It is everywhere, inside and outside me. We say body and soul. Do you say that too?

DOCTOR: No.

THERESE: What do you say then?

DOCTOR: Body is enough.

THERESE: Why?

DOCTOR: I do not believe there is a soul. You show it to me. – It is just a myth.

THERESE: But –

DOCTOR: Sorry, Sister, forget it. You were telling me about yourself. Do continue, please.

THERESE: I have forgotten, where I was.

DOCTOR: You were telling me about the pain in growing.

THERESE: Oh, yes, now I remember. – Suddenly all security was taken away. Darkness, total darkness descended on me *(gasps for breath)* and I was left hanging over the abyss. At first I did not know what was happening. It was like an ice cold hand gripping my soul. The fear was unbearable. I did not want to live and I did not dare to die. But as I was hanging there not knowing if I should fall – and fall where to? – or continue to hang on one thread, something strange happened. I saw life, all life, sinful and holy, beautiful and ugly, small and great, I saw into life, all life and it was one. – I entered into the minds of men – and I was one with all humanity – doubting, suffering; and what suffering there is! – I was one in all the vast multitude of all times and ages. I was everywhere and I was everybody. We were all one, and I loved everybody as I have never loved before. –

When I opened my eyes, I was no longer a child. I am still hanging over the abyss. It is still dark. But now I know that the thread is not going to break. The light will come. How I know, I do not know but, I know. If I did not somehow know this, I would not go on. – All this happened in a dialogue with God. – You may laugh, but this is how it happened. You can say I am silly or that it is my imagination. – But you cannot cancel it. You cannot eradicate God from my life. You would never understand me if you try to think of me without God. – I know that you do not believe. – I do. Why it is so, I do not know. But – I know now that the borderline between us is very thin. We all walk on the edge of the abyss. The same longing, the same anxiety is in our heart. In Zarathustra's too.

DOCTOR: What do you know about him? You have not read him, have you?

THERESE: I know him now.

DOCTOR: How did you get to know him?

THERESE: Aha! You would like to know that, do you not?

DOCTOR: Very much indeed.

THERESE: I have met him.

DOCTOR: Met him?

THERESE: I knew you would be surprised.

DOCTOR: But, Sister, Zarathustra is a fictive person.

THERESE: Are you sure?

DOCTOR: Of course I am.

THERESE: But we did meet.

DOCTOR: Where?

THERESE: You would not understand if I told you.

DOCTOR: Tell me anyway.

THERESE: On the brink of infinity. We gazed and we gazed until there was nothing more. We all gaze into infinity. It is frightening. It looks so empty – so you would say, it is empty – but I know – I know that God is there in the emptiness. *(Whispers.)* How I know? I cannot explain. –
God counts in my life. More so when He hides himself. – That is how I understand the unbelievers, the blasphemers too. I could have been one. I can sit with them in solidarity, in real comradeship, because we are all one. Do you see? The atheist is my brother. He is very close to me, much closer than many of the devout. Only those who have been out on the deep waters will know what I am talking about. Many of my sisters would think I am crazy saying things like these. Perhaps I am crazy, but if this is to be crazy I want to be crazy. You know, only when you stand there at the edge of the abyss and feel the surge, the pull down do you know what life is all about. – It – really was – only there – there that I met God. With the atheist I saw Him for the first time. God counts – But how different it all is from what I thought when I entered the convent!! I think that somehow He counts to every-body – Why would they deny Him otherwise?

DOCTOR: Why do you all the time refer to the unbelievers as they? I am not a believer.

THERESE: Sorry professor, wrong pronoun! – But I cannot think of you as a non-believer. Strange, is it not? – Perhaps because the border-line is so thin. Seeing you, I know we are the same. – All human hearts are the same. – Someone once showed me a great painting. I have for-gotten the name of the artist. He is a contemporary French artist. – You know, I am very interested in art. – It was fascinating. The horizon as it

were disappeared and with the artist you were drawn into the painting, further and further – into infinity. You just felt the pull. –
I must say something, because that is part of me too. You can say that it is childish, I do not mind, but everybody wants to have a mission in life. – And in that darkness and pain, when I was as it were delivered up to mysterious forces, in that dialogue with God, in that battle when childishness and selfishness – and I had a lot of it – was knocked off and I was left empty, naked, wounded and bleeding before Him – He was more real to me than ever – And I knew – I knew He wanted me to tell everybody – He was there. – He is there in the abyss. Infinity is not empty. To tell that is my mission and when I am dead you must tell that too. But do not let them forget that I was afraid. –

DOCTOR: You are an astonishing girl. It is a pity you die so young. Yes, I know you are already old, but according to the calendar you could have been going on for many more decades. Yes, it is a pity. It would have been interesting to see what would have become of you.

THERESE: Coming from you, that was not even cynical.

DOCTOR: How could I be cynical with you?

(Mother Gonzague returns.)

MOTHER GONZAGUE: I am sorry I was kept so long.

DOCTOR: Not at all, Mother. We have had a very interesting discussion.

MOTHER GONZAGUE: Really?

THERESE: We talked about God.

MOTHER GONZAGUE: God. There is nothing to say about Him. *(Turns to the doctor.)* So you have not examined her?

DOCTOR: There is no need for it at this stage Mother, unless her condition becomes really traumatic. I just keep an eye on the development of the sickness and her condition; and it has been quite steady for several days now.

MOTHER GONZAGUE: So, she is a little improved, then?

DOCTOR: No, Mother. At this stage there are no improvements and there will not be any.

MOTHER GONZAGUE: Can you not do anything, Doctor?

DOCTOR: No, Mother. She is beyond the help of medicine. We can only try to keep her comfortable and ease the pain. It is just a question of time now.

MOTHER GONZAGUE: Well, doctor, you do not give us much hope, do you?

DOCTOR: Would you like me to tell you a lie and deceive you? You of all people should be ready to face death honestly and openly. – Sister herself is, I think. *(Looks at Thérèse.)*

MOTHER GONZAGUE *(quickly)*: Yes, she is.
(Pause, during which a bird is heard singing outside.)

DOCTOR *(picks up his bag)*: Good bye for now. I will be back tomorrow. Check her temperature, Mother, and let me know immediately if there is a drastic change.

MOTHER GONZAGUE: Certainly, Doctor.

(They leave the room.)

DOCTOR *(Stops, turns to Thérèse)*: Do not forget the book!

MOTHER GONZAGUE: Which book?

THERESE: Doctor Legrange wants to read one of St Teresa's books.

MOTHER GONZAGUE: Really??

THERESE: Which one would you recommend, Mother? I think her *Life* would be the best one, do you not?

MOTHER GONZAGUE: I suppose so.

(Exit Mother Gonzague and Doctor. Music. Black out.)

(Light on to Nietzsche in a small sparsely furnished room.
A street outside is visible through a window, on a small table
a rose in a vase. Nietzsche walks around writing.)

NIETZSCHE: It is night – I live in my own light, I drink the flames from my own inner fire – It is night: ah that I must be the light! And thirst for night! And loneliness! – It is night – *(Light fades. Nietzsche continues to walk writing and readying.)* This is my hand. I, Friedrich

Nietzsche exist here and now with this hand. But how do I know that? How can I know that this is my hand? What if it is not? Ha, ha! You Friedrich, you have no hands. If you had, you would kill. Hands are to kill, to fight. – Who am I? – What is man? Man is an animal, one animal among many. Meow meow, bow bow. Do not say he is intelligent. Aristotle was wrong there, man is neither rational nor intellectual. Woman is a mistake of nature, yes, the old boy was right there at least. Even so, there is a difference. But what is the difference? He is neither angel nor animal. But what is he then? How can I explain it? Do I know? Perhaps he is a beast, yes, a beast! But when the beasts fight, super-man arises. Ah, that is it! What has brought about all great achievements of the human race? In society, in art, in knowledge? It has been brought about through power-struggle: fight and strife; a battle in which the strongest, the fittest survived and won. Life is nothing but a fight. History proves it. You kill or you are killed. The strongest conquer, and will conquer and conquer again until we have created the super-man. – Anything man does he does because he wants power. The Will to power is the essence of man. *(Music.)* The will to power is the root to all great accomplishments of man all through history. Look at the Greeks, look at the Romans. Look at a country, look at a city, at a family, at an individual. What drives them on? Never mind what they say. Few have got the courage and the honesty to say it, but they practise it. There is nothing but the will to power that drives them on. They would not live otherwise. Will power; fight for it or die. You will not be happy, unless you dominate, dominate somebody at least. The ruler dominates the people. The husband dominates his wife – and she the children, and the children one another. – And if you have nobody else to dominate, you dominate the dog. To discipline the dog is but to exercise you will to power – at least somebody is subject to you and you have power, if only over a brute animal; that is better than nothing. You have power and satisfaction. What about the teacher? Power over the pupils. That is what he wills – nothing else. The philosopher? Power over the minds of men. And what about the ascetic? The poor man has nothing left but his own body; so – he exercises his power. That satisfies him: power over his own body. Will to power – self satisfaction. Man is but will to power. Power, power nothing but power. *(He takes the vase with the rose, smashes the vase and tears the rose to pieces.)* You are no more. I have extinguished you, never more will you be. Be gone, be gone. This is all, there is nothing more to it. Do you want to hear? Nothing, nothing and Power. Power. –

But the world, this wretched world: a monster of energy, without beginning, without end; enclosed by "nothingness" as by a boundary; eternally self-creative, eternally self-destructive, without aim, unless the joy of the circle is itself an aim; do you want a name for this world? – A solution for all your riddles? This world is the will to power – and nothing besides! And you yourself are also this will to power – and nothing besides!

(Towards the end of this sentence we begin to hear a whip; a horse in the street is being whipped. Nietzsche catches sight of the scene, screams, rushes out, throws his arms around the neck of the horse.)

NIETZSCHE *(sobs)* My poor little horse! I love you. *(He loses consciousness, and falls to the ground. As he falls to the ground the most violent part of Movement 4 is being played. Blackout. Music continues for a while.)*

MOVEMENT FIVE

Nietzsche is alone on a bare stage.
Franziska Nietzsche enters with a glass of milk.

FRANZISKA NIETZSCHE: Would you like a glass of milk, Fritz.

NIETZSCHE: No.

FRANZISKA NIETZSCHE: I have got my little son back. Poor little Fritz, you came back to your mother in the end. Who could ever have imagined it would happen this way. God's ways are strange, sometimes too strange, but I have got you back, that is all that matters to me. Or is it really? I do not understand you, my boy. You have always been a stranger to me and yet I love you so much. Fritz, Fritz, do you hear me? Are you asleep already? *(Hums a lullaby.)* That day they brought you back, oh, it was terrible! Nobody could have recognized the great philosopher. My poor little Fritz, you really looked like a lunatic that day. No wonder Overbeck was upset. The poor man, I did not know which of you to pity most. But, then – you did not know anything, did you? Did you know? Sometimes I wonder – I wish I could read your mind and see what goes on there. Your sister says, I would be horrified. And yet she is so proud of you! I do not understand her either. I do not understand either of my children. It was all so much easier in the old days, when you were little, and your father was alive. I wonder what he would have said about all this. – The blasphemies – oh, no, it was terrible! He could not have meant it! is that why your mind had to go in the end? It was too great, and you went too far. I always feared something like this might happen. Perhaps it was the best. One day we will know. –You are safe now, my little son, back with your mother. I only pray to God that you may go before I do. Who would look after you if I were not here? They would nurse you, but they would not know that you are a little boy in a man's body. They would just say you were mad. I thought so too, when you wrote those horrible books. Why did you write them? No, you cannot answer. It is better so. It is better this way. *(Exits.)*

NIETZSCHE *(calls after her)*: Mother.

FRANZISKA NIETZSCHE: I thought you were asleep.

NIETZSCHE: No.

FRANZISKA NIETZSCHE: What is it then, my boy?

NIETZSCHE: Mother, was my father a pious man?

FRANZISKA NIETZSCHE: Hm – yes, I think so.

NIETZSCHE: Why do you hesitate?

FRANZISKA NIETZSCHE: I just had not thought of it that way – but – yes, he was. – We did not talk about these things. You performed your religious duties. It was part of life. – And he was also quite a lot older than I.

NIETZSCHE: So you never challenged him?

FRANZISKA NIETZSCHE: There was no need for it, Fritz. I believed what he believed.

NIETZSCHE: Bourgeois Christianity!

FRANZISKA NIETZSCHE: Do not be sarcastic, Fritz! You used not to be cynical and you idolized your father when you were a boy.

NIETZSCHE: And one day, one day I wanted to give you a rose, - but now, now I have seen too much, mother.

FRANZISKA NIETZSCHE: Sometimes I wish I had not sent you to boarding school. It all seemed to go wrong there. You got such queer ideas into your head. – Before that you were a pious and devout boy.

NIETZSCHE: I started to use my brain, mother. Does not even your Paul say that when he was a child he used to think like a child, but when he had grown up he put away what was childish?

FRANZISKA NIETZSCHE: You have got an astonishing knowledge of Scripture. – Childish and childlike are not the same thing.

NIETZSCHE: Can one be childlike without being childish? – Is that possible?

FRANZISKA NIETZSCHE: I think so, Fritz.

NIETZSCHE *(Looks at her, says nothing for a while, then, no longer lucid, begins to sing on a monotonous tune)*: Think so, think so – think so – *(he becomes restless. Franziska walks up to him and cuddles him until he is calm again, then leaves the stage.)*

NIETZSCHE *(sits still for a while)*: We have been here before, you and I, and we will come back. I sat in this same chair and I will sit in it again, the same chair. You too sat in the same chair last time and you will sit there the next time and the next – and the next – Everything will be the same: the same chair, the same clothes, the same room, the same evening; outside too it will all be the same: the same street, the same house, the same sky, the same weather, the same darkness

– the same as it was that other time, and the time before, and the time before. It all comes back again and again; everything the same, not better not worse either, just the same, there is no fulfillment, no meaning, no arrival, just repetition – round and round, again and again. *(He begins to draw a circle in the air with his right hand; a monotonous slow movement that gradually slows down.)* Again – and again, and again – and again – there is no way out – again, again. *(Music from the 5th Movement. He moves his hand slower and slower until the music begins to work itself up to a crescendo, then the hand moves faster and faster in bigger circles. At the final "key-clash", it forcefully drops onto his knee, and he sinks down. He sits immoveable, music stops with the rest after the "key-clash". Blackout.)*

(Light onto Thérèse in bed in the same infirmary as in the 4th Movement but more sparsely furnished. On each side of the bed Mothers Agnes and Gonzague are kneeling. Thérèse is restless, struggling for breath and relief. Every word she says is laboured and uttered with great difficulty in a gasp.)

THERESE: It – it – is dark – so dark – but the – tunnel – is – soon – ended – it – must – be – and then – there is – light – there – must be – light – on the – other – side – I believe – I do – believe – Oh – is there no death for me – only suffering – the cup – is filled – filled to the brim – but – I shall drink it – Oh – good Jesus – I drink – with You – for all – *(Pause during which the struggle for breath gets worse.)*
Are you there? – Answer me! *(Clasping her crucifix.)* Oh, it is pure suffering – no help – *(She struggles to say something for a long time.)* I – so alone – so alone, Oh Good Virgin – help me – *(Clasping her crucifix, whispers)* I believe, I believe. – *(Slowly she relaxes, her face becomes serene as she sinks back into her pillows.)*

THERESE *(raising herself up, smiling)*: Jesus, I love you. *(Kissing her crucifix she sinks back into her pillows.)*

(The Resurrection motif from the 5th Movement begins.
Light fades to total blackout.)

Curtain opens. Nietzsche on the stage, in the same position
as in previous scene. Thérèse enters, dressed in white,
with her veil flying round her head, stops at a
short distance from Nietzsche, who does not see her.

THERESE: Bon Jour, Monsieur Nietzsche.

NIETZSCHE *(startled)* : Who are you ?

THERESE: Do you not remember me ?

NIETZSCHE: I do not know you.

THERESE: Of course, you do.

NIETZSCHE: Are you French?

THERESE: As you please.

NIETZSCHE: Who are you?

THERESE: You know me. –

NIETZSCHE: You, again! What do you want?

THERESE: I have come to fetch you.

NIETZSCHE: Fetch me? What for?

THERESE: But we agreed.

NIETZSCHE: I do not know what you are talking about. We have never met.

THERESE: Of course we have. Are you coming with me or not?

NIETZSCHE: To where, if I may ask?

THERESE: You ask so many questions.

NIETZSCHE: I have hardly said anything.

THERESE: Not now, that is true. Are you coming?

NIETZSCHE: To where?

THERESE: To the Parnassus.

NIETZSCHE: Are you Greek now?

THERESE: As you please.

(Pause, during which music.)

THERESE: Come, then.

NIETZSCHE: I am not wont to go with unknown ladies.

THERESE: Come on, do not pretend.

NIETZSCHE: Why should I come with you?

THERESE: Because I love you.

NIETZSCHE: No woman has ever loved me.

THERESE: I love you.

NIETZSCHE: I do not believe you.

THERESE: Why can you not believe me ?

NIETZSCHE: Women always lie.

THERESE: I do not. I promised you to come back and I did.

NIETZSCHE: That is different.

THERESE: Why is it different?

NIETZSCHE: Do not ask such stupid questions.
THERESE: You did not believe I should come back, did you?

NIETZSCHE: No, I did not.

THERESE: There, you see.

NIETZSCHE: See what?

THERESE: That I did not lie.

NIETZSCHE: Does it matter?

THERESE: Yes, it matters much.

NIETZSCHE: Why?

THERESE: Because – You did not believe I should come back and I did. So why can you not believe I love you?

NIETZSCHE: Because no woman has ever loved me.

THERESE: Your mother ?

NIETZSCHE: That is different.

THERESE: There, you see.

NIETZSCHE: Why should you love me?

THERESE: I love you because I love you. Do you not understand?

NIETZSCHE: What do you get out of it?

THERESE: Love.

NIETZSCHE: So that you can have power over me?

THERESE: May I?

NIETZSCHE: I knew that was what you wanted.

THERESE: You do not understand.

NIETZSCHE: I think I do, my lady. And nobody, least of all a woman, is going to have power over me. I know your trickery.

THERESE: No, you do not.

NIETZSCHE: I see. You think you are clever. Would you then explain to me what love is.

THERESE: I cannot explain. But I love you.

NIETZSCHE: I do not love you.

THERESE: Of course you do.

NIETZSCHE: No, I do not love, I have never loved, and I will never love.

THERESE: I know you love.

NIETZSCHE: I do not love. And I will never love.

THERESE: I will show you how to love. Do not look like that. It is not as you think.

NIETZSCHE: What is it then, Mademoiselle?

THERESE: Come with me and you will know.

NIETZSCHE: To where?

THERESE: To the mountains.

NIETZSCHE: Do you like mountains too/

THERESE: Of course.

NIETZSCHE: What will we do there?

THERESE: Walk and walk, see the sunrise, the clouds –

NIETZSCHE: Not the sunset?

THERESE: That too. All is there.

NIETZSCHE: What else will we do?

THERESE: Breathe the air and hear the birds –

NIETZSCHE: And sing the fleeting moments of time.

THERESE: Time is gone.

NIETZSCHE: Recurrence, recurrence -

THERESE: No, come and see –

NIETZSCHE: You stay, stay here.

THERESE: Come and see the cherry blossom.

NIETZSCHE: It is better to stay under the oak.

THERESE: Come and pick cherries with me. They are ripe now.

NIETZSCHE: Let them fall.

THERESE: No, we must pick them, come.

NIETZSCHE: No, you stay, – stay with me.

(Short pause.)

THERESE: Can we not go together?

NIETZSCHE: What do you want?

THERESE: If we go together, we can pick the roses too.

NIETZSCHE: And prick ourselves.

THERESE: There are no thorns.
NIETZSCHE: You lie, like all cowards; just trying to please. A rose without thorns?

THERESE: Yes.

NIETZSCHE: Where are they?

THERESE: The thorns?

NIETZSCHE: Yes.

THERESE: In us.

NIETZSCHE: Ludicrous.

THERESE: You do not believe me?

NIETZSCHE: Not for one moment.

THERESE: That makes me sad.

NIETZSCHE: You are soft. – A rose without thorns is a lie and for the weak and cowardly.

THERESE: Not now.

NIETZSCHE: I will only pick roses with thorns.

THERESE: Why do you want to hurt yourself?

NIETZSCHE: The thorns make you strong.

THERESE: Only if you pick the flowers gently.

NIETZSCHE: The strong must not be gentle.

THERESE: Why not?

(Violin music.)

NIETZSCHE: What else will we do in your garden?

THERESE: Play the violin.

NIETZSCHE: You play too?

THERESE: Hm.

NIETZSCHE: What are we going to play?

THERESE: Duet.

NIETZSCHE: Who plays first?

THERESE: Aha! –

NIETZSCHE: I cannot play.

THERESE: Why?

NIETZSCHE: The strings are broken.

THERESE: Never mind.

NIETZSCHE: I cannot play.

THERESE: You can.

NIETZSCHE: You do not play better than I do.

THERESE: No, you are the better player.

NIETZSCHE: You cannot play with broken strings.

THERESE: If you bend they will not break.

NIETZSCHE: They are broken already.

THERESE: Never mind.

NIETZSCHE: Are your strings broken too?

THERESE: No.

NIETZSCHE: Why not?

THERESE: You see, when I could not get it I did not try to tighten the strings, I just slackened them.

(Music.)

NIETZSCHE: Slackened them –

THERESE: Come and play –

NIETZSCHE: No, I cannot –

(Curtain.)

THERESE: Come, – come

NIETZSCHE: Stay, – stay

(This dialogue will continue softer and softer until it dies out.)

END

"To every man his death."
(Martin Heidegger)

Drama in five movements.
Music: Gustav Mahler's 10th Symphony

Bridget Edman OCD